Clay
Cup

Lorraine Bruno Arsenault

Clare Songbirds Publishing House Poetry Series
ISBN 978-1-957221-06-9
Clare Songbirds Publishing House
Clay Cup © 2023 Lorraine Bruno Arsenault

Printed in the United States of America
FIRST EDITION

140 Cottage Street
Auburn, New York 13021
www.claresongbirdspub.com

You say you can't create something original? Don't worry about it. Make a cup of clay so your brother can drink.

~*Rumi*

Acknowledgments

A large part of how I live my life is grounded in gratitude. With that in mind I'd like to thank each of the following for publishing earlier versions of these works: *Chicken Soup for the Soul Miraculous Messages from Heaven* for "In the Light," *Chicken Soup for the Soul Touched by an Angel* for "Message from Michael," *The Healing Muse* for "Fall Morning," *Comstock Review* for "Archer of Lipstreams," and *In the Company of Women an Anthology Commemorating the 90th Anniversary of the CNY Branch of the NLAPW* for "Fragile Vessel"

A big thank you to Rachael Z. Ikins who both loves and lives poetry and encouraged me to organize these poems for publication and who continues to encourage me to keep writing; to Tish Dickinson, Canastota Writers Group for the many prompts she brought to our table, seeds that grew into poems; to Canastota Public Library Director Elizabeth Metzger who makes space for the art of writing to thrive in our community; to Michael Czarnecki of Foothills Publishing for encouraging me to believe I do have time to write; to Betsy Anderson, Teresa Gilman, Michael Sickler, Lou Buttino, Rachael Guido deVries and Craig Czury, my poetry muses who were inspiration for many of the poems here within; to Len Germinara and his critique group for helping with just the right changes; to Philip Arsenault for sharing the story about Michael Arsenault. And to the very nice lady in the Sacramento Poetry Center ZOOM who asked where she might read my poetry.

Many thanks to all yoga students and teachers who have allowed me to share the profound practice of yoga with them, and to Francois Raoult for lighting the way.

A very special thank you to Clare Songbirds for the opportunity to publish this collection.

Table of Contents

I dedicate this collection to my family--Joel, Elise, Ariana, Brady and Bobby, for their love, encouragement, and for having taught me more about living than I ever imagined.

Part I

A Nomad Walking Among Poets

"It was at that age, that poetry came in search of me."

~Pablo Neruda

About Writing

She told the group, "Lorraine, she lives in her head."
She said it like it was not the ideal.
I sat there wondering why that was a bother.
"What if I do?" I thought, "that is where the words are
all the beautiful words streaming in alphabet rivers,
rolling down aerie slopes tumbling one after the other
cavorting like puppies at play.
They float like satellites navigating among stars,
burst forth from darkness like sparkling fountains
of exploding fireworks bringing light.
They nudge and brush against each other dashing about
like children playing tag.
They sail like white triangles touched by sunbeams.
I roll my tongue around their sounds
just to listen to them,
to hear how they make me feel—
ripe and juicy some,
others, pure like bells ringing in icy air.
Some are smooth and fragile like robins' eggshells,
or velvety with luxury like exquisite cashmere.
Others still are magical as sleight-of-hand,
woeful as the song of mourning doves,
cutting like a sharp knife's edge.
They have power these words
to raise the soul
to quicken the heart
to well the eyes with tears.
So what if I live in my head. The words are there,
beautiful words in rivers of alphabets
just waiting for me.

Fragile Vessel

She walked through the door holding herself together
as one might hold a cracked pot working to keep
soil from seeping through the opening.
She struggled to conceal the fissure,
careful not to let what was inside out.
She let her coat slip from her shoulders in measured
time,
relieved her feet from her shoes,
slowly navigated passage across the room.
The cleft widened more with each deliberate footstep,
exposed bits of her she labored to conceal.
She reached us, freer, let go for not being able to hold
on—
the vessel then split wide open.
Without warning, clumps of old pain, stones of abuse,
mold-crusted disappointments
tumbled from her on to the floor—
a few at first, then many more wet with tears
poured out in the muted glow of twilight.
It started years ago, a way of easing hurt—
a glass of wine, a bottle maybe…every day
until she could hold no more.
We wrapped our arms around her like ropes
as to set a seal to fasten her pieces whole.
Empty, there was room now to fill
with new clean earth, water, sunshine, seeds of hope.

Yoga Teacher

Mother's doll was a stick
she dressed in leaves and flowers.
She taught me to give my heart to
the humblest thing.

My dolls were of vinyl
I dressed in cotton and voile.
They let me bestow my love upon
idyllic things.

I left my mother's house
dressed in ivory and lace.
draped my dolls in tissue sealed tight in
attic boxes.

I birthed two babies—girls
I dressed in smocking and bows,
hugged them close until they showed me
how to let go.

Dolls fashioned of flesh and
bone come to me now. They ask
me to bend their legs, stretch their arms
make their spines long.

I do. Joints unlock. Mus-
cles loosen, minds relinquish. Tears
weep from secret wounds form streams.
to the ocean.

Sonam's Magic Box
Dedicated to Sonam Targee 11/25/1956 –4/15/2022

That January night long ago,
submerged alone among strangers
in a large, darkened room foreign to me,
treading swelling tides of grief,
my eyes fixed on a window of snow flurry
lit like crystal sparks in a flush of streetlamp.
A latch clicked.
He was late, the one we waited for,
the one to sit lotus to our lotus,
to complete our circle.
Sonam dashed across floorboards
in barefoot quick-step pianissimo
joyful of case tucked beneath his arm.
He settled at the foot of a trinity of
sculpted golden Buddhas
stilled in candlelit meditation,
unlocked his case, unveiled his harmonium,
gently invited air into its lung…
inhale, exhale, i-n-h-a-l-e, e-x-h-a-l-e…
Sonam's fingers shifted deftly over
keys black and white
freeing the organ's prana…
Notes like huge, winged birds
flowed out in ecstasy soaring,
merging into every heartbeat.
Sonam chanted sacred mantras
setting us to sail staves of musical flight
over mystical rivers, currents of bliss.
Oh, how we yearned to prolong our rhapsody
yet felt what was to come in each waning exhale…
the gentle let down of the last vibration quieted,
the final flutter of wing coming to land.
The stillness was deafening.

Corpse Pose

Practice was intense—
the warrior, half the moon, the pigeon
met me at my edge.
I lay my spine along the bolster
ready for earth's invitation
I surrendered...
opening arms, giving weight to legs
stilling dancing thoughts
sinking, sinking, sinking...
no borders, no boundaries
mind, body, spirit
dwelling in some profound place
hazy it was—I struggled to see
a pool of water
my birth? my tears? rebirth?
reaching, reaching, reaching...
please...
a little closer...
a little clearer...
"Gently bring your awareness
back to your bodies," she interrupted,
vanishing the water
leaving me yearning for
yet another glimpse

Elegant Rhapsody

Sound-wave stevedores
unload heart's heavy cargo
making room for a delivery of
bliss
It moves from black spheres,
low and sultry,
whispering
softly, sweetly from a slow dance
escalating as it picks up rhythm
swelling ecstatic.
Twirling tones from clefs and staffs
merge into chords swaying euphoric.
Melody entwines harmony,
together, they
ascend high across ceilings
glide against walls
tap windows
wend through doorways,
filling each empty space
with rapture.

Train Ride
   For Terry Plater

The train's chant "zoosha zoosha" roars up
from steel driving hard over steel,
wheels press against rails, mile after mile
exhaling each colon mark between abutted tracks.

Ghostly etchings appear across sky like apparitions of
transmission lines to a world beyond, but are unable to
bear messages or carry voices we can hear. Scenes flick by
exposing spent fields, specters of barns, a windowless
home.

There in the midst, deep shadow cradles a sunlake brilliant
with starfire melted into meadow bare of clouds pink
and gray
where hay flattens and mortals, warm and illumined,
plant seeds, watch rainfall, kick up earthdust.

We evolve, acting out our contracts with heaven
shifting back and forth between sun and moon, moving
from light to dark and back again until each joy-filled,
heart-wrenching detail is satisfied knowing the train
never stops.

Waiting for Words
for William Bruno

He stood at the door to leave
half in, half out
clad in black t-shirt, khaki shorts,
worn sandals baring toes.
He looked at me--
his face sad, and gray.
Was he saying,
"I'm sorry?"
"I have to go?"
"I wish it could be different?"

I waited for words
balanced taut
like deft acrobats
clinging to a high wire
stretched between us
working toward me,
balancing
yet never moving forward.

I sat at my desk
wanting among paper piles,
messages, mail littered about,
tethers pulling at me
phone ringing,
intercom sounding,
someone walking in
snapped the line
that connected us.

He turned, hampered,
his back to me
he walked through the door
to the other side
silently, alone
taking his words with him
leaving us each
half a rope.

Fall Morning
For Millie Bruno

October morning rises spare—
thin yellowed fingers,
loath to leave their cloudblanket,
slip a cool hand along
the back of a wide-eyed doe.
I stand at wood's edge
shadowed in the last of night,
eye-to-eye with the deer.
Alert to the heckle of a crow's caw,
she bends her head,
lifts her heels,
leaps away. And I?
I slip into a dark maze
of slick black tree trunks.
Treebones crack against my legs,
leafpalms slide beneath my soles,
earthhollows beg at my feet.
I find her there again—
not her face—but her fear
when September last
dropped her in a midnight forest,
stilled her voice,
deadened her limbs,
left her jeweled eyes
to peer through forest murk.
I fall by her side, offer warmth,
watch as a lone ray sifts through
tangled boughs, touches her heart,
gathers her light back to the sun.

Unyoked

She lay prostrate,
a landed dove flesh belly to earth,
arms to sides, palms down, eyes closed.
She listened for the memory of ocean
within her shell,
rode ancient waves
through
incarnations spent
searching for one event—
Promises to Keep...

She recited again,
"I take the vows of
chastity, poverty, obedience,
and to be the bride of Christ"
for this lifetime"
and added
"this lifetime only."

Bondage loosened
set free for the rest of time—
Bells chimed, pealed thin,
fragile with age,
rolled from her tongue
fled her mouth.
tumbled out of her,
shattered to dust.

Zoe's Dream

The years lock Zoe's joints stiff;
no sheep to herd, no children to guard,
    back leg quivering, she walks to her place
        in the cool dark cavern of spruce boughs
          to feign her watch.
Secretly nestled in shadow, she closes her eyes enters
        a magical place between sleeping and waking.
Youth calls her to fields wide and green
      where the white cat stalks mice and moles.
She runs free and lithe, paws paddling air
      in quick subdued fury. Stifled barks rise like
    tiny whimpers
from her evergreen sanctuary.
      Over knolls, through meadows,
          she chases prey.
At last, her body stills, her panting fades.
Tiny lapping sounds tell she's found
a cool, clear stream to drink from.
Her muzzle loosens,
      Satisfied, she rests as I watch her,
        questioning what is real, what is dream…

My Shepherd

The black dog begs of me.
to tread on morning's snow diamonds.
He lifts his paws from icy patches,
burrows a nose in silvery drifts,
sniffs out mice-trails below white dunes,
shakes a powdery mask from his snout.

The black dog begs of me
to slip through blue shadows in freezing night.
He leads me through frosty corridors,
perks his ears to a coyote's howl,
halts astonished in stillness shattered,
looks back to make certain I am there.

The black dog begs of me.
to look ahead to windows streaming gold.
He pulls me along a hoar-jagged course,
brings me at last to home's yearned-for-hearth,
curls in a ball at my frost-worn feet,
heaves the bass of a satisfied sigh.

Found

Wandering from forest, she came upon a shore,
a boy tugging a kite string, hope amusing sky.
She watched bemused, brushing trail from her shoes,
bits of broken bells, flecks of hearts, dewdrops of tears.

Sun seeped down dripping red from her hair.
Shells, tattered by restless tides wave-tossed to
earth's lip, poked through sand pierced her feet,
made her howl fist-to-sky

Scraps of light sparked through dusk touched
a hazel twig fingers holding tight.
It sang like a flute without holes,
spiraling melodies upward from her core.

A nod to Pablo Neruda

All That Glitters

We were in the '48 Ford
he bought her to drive us to
buy groceries, visit family,
go to the doctor.
She pressed a little more on the brake,
eased the car into our garage,
her dark hair slipping from the sun
when a spark from the floor touched my eye.
I leaned over, held up a rhinestone earring.
Her face fell into my lap, it lay there flat, colorless.
"It's not mine," she said
and seven-year-old me knew…
It happened after last night's show,
after that woman's voice
slid gold notes through the mike over to him
after her gold hair flickered in the spot light,
after a flash of her earring took his eye,
that's when my mother fastened another button
over her heart.

Before the Frost

I wanted to go apple picking, idle around in sunshine,
wander down country roads...

We drove to the lake house instead, to shut water off,
drain pipes, lock summer up inside.

I found the cottage cold, full of damp nights and fusty
stillness of warmer days spent.

I set out to dismantle lamps, wrap bowls in plastic,
pack sheets and pillows away.

Mice had moved in, thought us gone, left droppings on
slipcovers, in a cupboard with the wine.

I pitched open the lakeside door, tempted warmth inside,
drew in the tang of spice and pine.

A gust of air set a yellowed leaf adrift,
floating it in to rest by a dining chair.

Geese squawked, wings and legs a-splash,
perturbed by a lone boat's final pass.

Two butterflies fidgeted along shore, settled on a rock,
took wing from water's edge.

I fixed my eyes west on red sky,
observed color drain from hills

watched the last glitter of sunlight fade,
hungered for an apple.

Poet's Picnic

I watched her like an expectant child
a magician revealing each trick
carefully drawn from the shoulder tote
she held heartclose.

With a flourish,
flap and flutter of checkered cotton,
red and white flirted with light and shadow
settled softly, sighing,
content to drape over cedar picnicplanks

Linen squares rescued from a rubbish bin
laundered bleach clean, lay bare palest memoirs
of repasts long ago,
sweet sprays of pinkyellowblue flowers
embroidered in corners
exact, precise, correct,
folded neatly around parsley sprigs and apricot jam
slipping past crusty borders of rye
and tonguesticking almond butter
thickspread for substance.

We sipped dry cold wine.

She tossed me a handful of words,
bright colored playthings
skipping and bouncing between us,
we turned them this way and that
linked them together like traincars
took them apart like watchgears
pitched them back and forth
cars, gears turning to shapes and colors
bits of magical verse
poems
held wonderingly open to the sun
marveling at their very alchemy

We took them with us
on the hiking trail

handheld them down steep stone steps
brushing through pine boughs,
over dirt and stones
swaying with them to breezesong,
letting sundust settle on them
beneath gauzy leafveil
where creek waters freefell from rocky edges
noisy and raucous, tumbling, bursting,
splashing down across our palms
rushing our words into streams
merging and wending
nourishing forestgreen.

Independence Day Observing

We sat on worn decking
at an old storage building
its windows boarded up
like eyes blinded,
pressed our backs
against its face of
wooden clapboards
shedding paint chips
like skin flaking from flesh.

We spread the flowers
of our cloth
over old footsteps,
poured wine
into plastic stemware
ate felafels off melamine.

We reverberated to
heart-thumping
crescendos of Sousa's
Stars and Stripes
marching toward us
from a distance.

We shook with each
brilliant explosion of sound
as if it were gunfire
thundering over
the nearby lake
echoing against the City.

We held the dance of
light shards bursting
heavenward
in our eyes,
dazzled by neon colors
outshining summer stars
falling toward us quickly
fading in their descent,

absorbed into night
their spell painted
on every face.

We watched a moving stream
of families festive, babbling
flow from the inner harbor
to idle frustrated
in lines of dammed up traffic.

Life's Souvenirs

Time and again we dust off our keepsakes,
place them around us like crown jewels,
admire them, take them for granted.

Framed prints, a straw hat, a pot your aunt gave you,
flatware, two blue handwoven rugs,
a mosaic lamp your child made in grade school.

They hung on walls, rested in drawers,
stood on tables, protected the kitchen floor—
you barely were aware of their presence.

He drove to the lake cottage that early spring day
passed rivulets of melted snow, eager for summer.
He phoned just before dinnertime, his voice controlled.

He said the windowed door you draped in lace
lay in shards over the floor clubbed to a gaping hole
open to wind, rain, your fear.

Those things you thought were yours are gone,
not given, but Taken, Stolen Robbed—the coffee table,
a photo of the cottage in winter,
your safety, peace of mind— gone.

Is this how it is to be raped, to be penetrated in violence,
trust shattered into slivers scattered dead over tiles,
the notes of your heartsong dislodged, burgled away?

Where are those trinkets that gave your haven solace—
the Amish sewing box from which you stitched tears,
candles that gave light to the dark; who has them now?

Why?

Reunion

A long walk up old stairs,
soft rasp of slipper over wood,
the turning of a knob,
a held breath.
He lay in the attic
asleep between sheets of typeface char
tapped onto onion skin
covered in Camus' ink dust.
Whispers of old folk songs,
chants of Viet Nam protest
beat against her ears.
"War is no place for a poet he wrote."
Hands dropped from clockface
Stars crossed skies undiscovered…
…he slipped between sunsets.
What could've been
fused in fate's womb
in a winter when marrow splintered
in the cold of it.
A phone call
footsteps through icy snow,
a long walk up old stairs,
a bowl of warm soup shared

The News 2017

There it goes, look at it roll!
My poor head
cracked open,
splintered into skullshards
spilling out photos and soundbytes
of white supremacists pulling triggers
politicians drooling mud
hearts, black and white, drowning in blood
terrorists
exploding bombs, exploding words
fake news, actual news.
I steady Sisyphus's rock
pushing it up the hill yet again
steep and slippery
my ears bleed,
my feet go numb
my arms quiver with the weight of it.
And then
my head fell off.

Red

Red is Offred's oppression,
a dress holding her heat, marking who she is,
or rather who they want her to be.
It is her blood they desire, the one she births
to commanders' wives.
She wonders of Cardinals and kings,
who stand in the sun in red robes of power.
Is it the moon that makes her red less?
She calls to Hester and the Magdalene,
thousands of red-dressed sisters follow,
a flowing march through the streets,
"I wear the red of power", Offred sings,
"Me too", each voice rings out,
like bells through the mountains

Map of Encounter

She paints
with deliberate acrylic strokes
an odyssey of her soul's incessant journey,
its aimless wanderings along elected pathways
over bridges of epiphanies and calamities.
She records a diary of traversing the ether
pushing through layers of self,
groping through dark, rejoicing in light,
She finds at the very center of being
her eyes, like a mirror luminous and ablaze,
reflecting back at her.

Lock Down Naples, FL

We took a walk last evening, the black dog and I,
through the city past sealed doors of boutiques,
art galleries, gift shops, eateries.

Windows tossed patches of light at our feet
like postcards written home of the fun we had had,
No buzz of traffic, no human cacophony, no one

but a lone young woman playing a violin,
her wistful chords meandering tenderly
through dark silky air.

We climbed aboard her notes sailing far beyond
touching stars, weaving moonbeams,
dancing the slow dance.

A flotilla of teens rushed by running us aground,
their voices spewing wind
overturned our boat.

We bailed for a side street lured to quietude,
its inky pitch enveloping us, sheathing us
in warm, womblike silence.

That's when I heard it, a forgotten ancient chant
sung from the stillness of my soul...I heard
the soft velvet sound of my own footsteps.

February 24, 2022

Grueling times for those in Ukraine. I wonder
how she is, the woman who made a coat for me…
I found her on Etsy last year, a face not visible to me.
I ordered coats from stores we know,
returned them after they arrived—
no lining, cheap fabric, skimpy to wear.
I thought "Ukraine knows winters like I do,
bone-chilling to the marrow."
I asked the woman if her design was warm,
with room for sweaters to be worn.
Her message was," yes, insulation veiled within."
I emailed measurements, US dollars,
worried over the agreement we made.
She wrote she had much sewing to do,
"Christmas, you know,
by New Year it will arrive to you."
"Fine" I answered, "I've no place to go,
a pandemic you know."
I waited weeks as they came and waned
to receive the effects of my gamble.
At dusk one day where snow built up
on a step outside my door,
I saw a brown box modest and square,
with tags showing customs postponed it.
I brought it in, cut its tape, released
the contents inside.
Fold upon fold, made to look small,
lay my custom-made camel coat.
I slid my arms into silky sleeves
feeling the weight of the wool,
I wear it to the office, to restaurants
and think of the woman who made it for me.
Is she crouched in some underground corner?
Are troops shooting at her, shelling her home?
Is she holding her sewing machine to shield herself?
Will Maria be cold?

Strings Attached

It used to be she'd arrive—or leave—
breezily planting a kiss on my cheek.
That was before the invader sneaked in,
the one we could not see,
soundless waiting to strangle our breath.
We were instructed not to touch our face,
for your face not to touch my face and
to wipe clean your presence with alcohol,
maybe then we'd be saved.
It might not be us stacked jenga-like
in refrigerated trucks
sorrow weeping rivers onto streets
flowing to vacant funerals.
Two years pass, we stand apart
suspicion commanding the air between us
the kiss locked in our eyes craving from stiff bodies.
Six feet apart, feet planted,
we smile, we nod, we ponder hope—
my daughter and I,
suspended marionettes living

Honing the Art

You left me by the creek
listening to the music of words,
laboring to eke their spirits from stones
not knowing how to hear them
and write poetry at the same time

Night Music

I hear
your footsteps in the hall,
the creak of door closing—
you're home.
The burdens of our day
ease,
night noises
are music to my ears.

Bits and Bytes

"How is he?" I ask my friend
who is his friend,
who I happened upon one Springday
in the bookstore's parking lot.
.
"How is he, our teacher,
the one who recalls countless words
from poets whose names
I've yet to discover,

the one who tutored us
in Kennings and Oulipo,
showed us there are poems
in Chinese images painted on porcelain lamps?"

"He's well," she says.
"Seems to have recovered fully
from a stroke…
He's writing again."

I wonder over the gigabytes
his heady hard drive holds,
his operating system of fluid access on command,
the word sculptures he recites at will.

I consider my hardware, the one
that seems ever full of bugs,
illegal actions, the one
lacking in RAM or ROM or both.

I catch bits of data trickling
from my eyes, ears, corners of my mouth,
I feel it leap from my hands, splat
onto tarmac, bounce and bob about.

I am bewildered how to retrieve it,
how to clean-uninstall what I no longer need,
update software, search engine vendors
who sell flash drives for my brain.

Archer of Lip Streams

Alphabet fletcher
you rouse mischief sparking bane of wood
drawing from the glory of elves
beating stone upon stone
whetting edge
to fasten broadhead to bowtell;
you mark love's shepherds
for their slaughter dew
with sweet aim
as you draw back your bow
letting fly feathers of book staff
to pierce where there is no bone.

Earth Stepper

Bone house angled within bone house,
impelled to course
riding through the roaring brides of ocean
to draw a first searing breath
in pure white brilliance;
howl charged in full timbre
as feet dangled searching for sundials
wandering into the anarchy of time.

Pearls

Honor is stark white—
its halos waltz on dazzling faces
connecting jewels of Indra's net,
pearls of infinite reflection
—I as you, you as me—
Replicating through creation
we who mirror the
mind.

Raga for Auntie

"Auntie, you vanting to haf de tea?"
"No thank you."
She sank into the old charpoy, belly up,
like a starfish tossed by ocean's exhale
blue cotton rippling around her,
sunfingers playing along her dress.

"Auntie, you vanting to haf de foodt?"
"No thank you."
The verandah cradled her,
seawaves pitching her, rocking her
between light and shadow
nudging stone walls
that braced earth from water.

"Auntie, some ting being de proh blem?"
"No problem."
Voices bumped against her,
images unraveling,
smoke unfurling from puja,
children tugging her sleeve,
an old seer boring her soul.

"Auntie vhat you be do ingk?
"I am writing."
Mango dribbled sweet from her palm,
trickled down to
laundry bleaching on dirt,
curry filling her lungs,
puchka retching her gut.

"Auntie, you be likingk India?'
"India?"
Human currents of rainbow flowed
pouring out,
voices, sitars, screeching scooters,
oil of sandalwood pervading,
rose petals skimming her toes...
India?
India awakens me.

Zirafa

Along a band of Serengeti trail,
    majestically g a n g l i n g,
        gracefully swift
           a-small-herd-of-giraff g AL lo PS
over h-e-a-t—w-a-v-e-d grasslands.

    Long-Necked, Tall-Legged, they

    r o a m t h e g r e a t e x p a n s e ...
        pause
        to eat
        by
        stand of
        thorny
        acacia,

chew leaves from high branches as
 giant EYES survey

A fric a's v a s t s a v a n n a h...
             see
  W il de bee st,   an TE lope, z **eb** r a

grazing peacefully mindful of such fleshy tower's sentry of

    ((**man** LION *l e o* p *a* r *d* in secret waiting))
      c a l m eyes tell of ancient stories,
              reflect

golden sunrises

        blood-colored sunsets.

The Girl Who Sailed On

They gather under sultry sun
on the marina's terrace
lunching on fried fish.

Iced tea beads sweat
onto the table, sweat
glues thighs to chairs.

She calls them by their maiden names,
these girls who hide
behind their mothers' faces.

Their voices scuttle recklessly
knocking up against old boats,
bouncing like bobbers on the lake.

Old stories surface,
judgments are proclaimed,
a gale of gossip heels her starboard.

Laughter's wind collapses,
drops into the doldrums
of an empty dish.

She pulls up anchor, cruises beyond
a trio of trumpeter swans dipping for algae,
and boats nodding at their tethers.

Death in the Ming Dynasty

Dhao ming 's melody
wove among clouds
east of her lover's heart
in the season of wood,
in the time of cherry blossom.
Junjie chased his beloved's song
through wisp and billow of Ming sky
recounting her delicate hand tracing symphonies
of blue brushstrokes on white porcelain; her squirrel-
hair brushes striking out bristly scales on arching backs of
her Emperor's five-clawed dragons, imperial dragons
auspicious dragons whose breath roared gifts from
beastly saw-toothed mouths—vase-owner gifts of
wealth and happiness, luck, prosperity, long life, gifts
from the Emperor. Junjie rose from dream from the
shade of an old gingko, heaped to his back his only be-
longings Dhao ming's, silk sack filled with tea leaves,
five grains of rice and her brushes cushioned in peony
petals. Junjie stepped upon the road of long journey to
the five sacred mountains, like the
four-clawed mythical serpent
chasing the pearl.

Ocean

        haaaaaaaaaaaaaah,
the conch whispers,
        eternal echoes swirl and spiral,
    Rumi sings of the moon,
of silver surfing to shore,
       fawhoooooshhhhhh
fawhoooooooshhhhhh
      waves, whorls of salty sea, curl,
crest and fall one upon another
          fawhoooooooooshhhhhh
       fawhoooooooshhhhhh
    splashes and bribbles spray shimmering
    gray
    a froth of white on sparking sands sweet-talk
    toes,
undulate, sweet-talk toes, undulate...
           sail, how I long to sail...
long to swim
      the Ocean...

Winter's Wind

January's breath
    gathers and swells with icy fury
        tears through plains and hollows
           like an invisible army
             pillages trees
        compels branches naked
           forces each to bend and wail.

Ghoulish troops
    ransack moon-still snow fields,
        leave in their wake
        eddies of ghostly whorls
           twisting in dazed frenzy.

   .   Covert battalions race forth
           lash ice-coated whips against the house
            howl like coy dogs around corners
             batter windows,
                cry through cracks,
                    implore entrance.
Wolf-hungry legions
    prowl where I dwell
        stalk corners
           shove shrubs
             scratch at the door
             scour for openings,
              one opening
                to stir calm
                  lay waste serenity,
                drop dust
                  of another place on
           my table.

Remembrance

Memory is full of swords and dust, it's
as small as the world and as huge as alone,
adrift as a stranded star.

Rosa Katour sits in the dark
in broken days of a far-flung sun
in silence so deep it makes her heart pound.

She sits in a room by a faceless clock
lost in a labyrinth, oblivious
to where her curious journey began.

What is a woman without memory,
but a doll caught between realms.
What is time, but a wind that never dies…

Violets

She used to leave for Florida
or Italy, Australia, too
all worked up about the plane ride;
called me when she landed.

She left me the key
to open her door
to water her plants
to wipe the dust away for her return.

She departed, this last time
without her purse.
without a ticket,
without calling to say she arrived.

I stopped by today
where she lived
to water her violets
did not wipe the dust away.

In August

In August when the dog days of summer
end too quickly and night comes too soon,
I dress my children in hoodies,
leading them into the dark.
I walk them deep into an acre,
beyond shadowed arms of trees,
feeling cool droplets of dew,
blades of grass glueing to our feet.
I unfold a blanket, stretch corners wide,
bid spines to lay to earth.
Eyes queue in a twinkling row
reflect stars light years away.

We wait.

Airplane lights throb, satellites track,
remote suns glimmer from the Milky Way.
A bullfrog chorus chants from the pond
syncs with the rasp of a cicada choir.
A lullaby of train wheels click-clacks
faintly along steel rails, highway traffic whispers
like women sharing secrets.

"I see it!!" shatters the hush.

"There!"

A shooting star!

An instant blazing flash,
brilliant across jet-black expanse—
fleeting…
We hurry to pitch our wishes to it,
the ones we have been holding onto
like agates of gold,
begging heaven to make the catch.

Fishing

We drove from overnight at camp,
tiny three-year old man in car seat,
me at the steering wheel.
It was time to return him to his father.

A man cast out a line from his dock.
I offered," Your papa used to like to fish.
"I know, "he said. "My daddy told me.
I wish he didn't die."

Suddenly, he cried out anguished,
"I don't want my daddy to die!
I don't want you to die either, Auntie Raine!
Why does God have to have every body."

Saturday Night Live
For Cindy Bruno Kryzakala

She said she saw them
Saturday night, live
Millie and Rose and Gramma Stone
sitting around Nana's table,
Nana's table
where every week began
Sunday
painted red with
tomato sauce and wine
on aunts and uncles,
cousins and friends
seated elbow-to-elbow
circling worn mahogany borders
savoring
the blissful din curling
to a vapor of coffee aroma as
the last dish dried
was laid to rest
in the old metal cupboard.
Cindy saw them laughing
having a grand time
both our moms and Gramma Stone
wrapped warm in wisps
of Maxwell House mist
talking
wanting us to know
they're fine
She felt full, at peace,
made a dish for me
because it was Monday
and she saw them
Saturday night live.

Departures

January, we drive south,
struggle through snow squalls,
slide on iced highways,
wipe rain from the car's shield,
to a place where the sun is.

More than a thousand miles
behind us,
we roll into a parking lot,
lug our bags up a flight of stairs,
unbolt the door to a boxlike condo.

Here we dwell for winter,
where the sun is.
sharing half a closet,
two drawers each and one car.

May, we drive north
gripped in steamy air
past flowering trees,
branches with new leaves
to a place where the lake is.

More than a thousand miles
behind us,
we pull onto graveled road,
cart our bags over stones,
turn a key,
unlock the cottage door.

Here we lodge for summer
where the lake is
sharing half a closet,
three drawers each.

And so it is—
north to south, south to north,
repeating the cycle of chasing the sun
to the gulf, to the lake
denying ice its due.

Then I remember,
when we each had a whole closet,
our own cars; when we didn't mind
about where the sun is,
because we were busy making a living.

Home Again

I search the mist of my mother's eyes
for mornings
where my father's smile rests,
where her sons' tallness walks beside her,
where my daughters' dreams nap.

I swim the tears of my mother's eyes
for islands
where her sisters' gaiety feasts
where her brothers' wine stains linen,
where her children's wounds soothe with salve.

I dance the light of my mother's eyes
past shadows,
where her sturdy walls are scoured clean
where her sunlit kitchen teems with food,
where her table spills onto chairs gone empty

I read the lines of my mother's eyes
beyond words
where fathomless pools
mirror my image that is her image
that guides me home again.

If Not for Love

Who would choose life
if not for love?
Souls content in an ether place
labor to take their first searing breath
tendered by ecstasy's currency—
a smile conveyed,
a wink proffered
a kiss shared.
We merge into caresses
riding song waves only we hear
creating yet another to hold heart close
pulling tight as it yanks away
leaving raw the flesh it touched.
We reflect ourselves like mirrors
repeating to infinity
until one of us fades
behind life's partitioning veil
holding fast with warm-cold fingers
slipping to that other plane
only to choose breath again.

Part II

Dancing by the Veil

Sleeping or waking we hear not the airy footsteps of the strange things that almost happen.

~Nathaniel Hawthorne

The first time I remember it happening was when I saw the white gauzy specter of my grandfather's face in the opened door of my dark closet the night before he passed on. I was a few days short of six.

Trust the Process

One day several years ago, I was invited to my friend Martha's house to meet her friend and Reiki mentor, Murray visiting from Missouri.

Reiki is an energy healing technique that promotes stress reduction, enhances relaxation and helps to reduce anxiety. It can bring on a meditative state as practitioners gently allow their hands to hover over a body in order to transmit energy. This energy works to improve balance and flow of organ and energy systems to support the body's own healing processes.

Martha and I were trained in the practice, but as we worked with more and more people, questions arose from our experiences using the technique. We were finding Reiki to be a profound energy practice. I shouldn't have been surprised that as we sat chatting at Martha's table, my hands felt vibration, my heart area felt heat. I was beginning to feel something special was present.

Martha was generous with her guest. I had the opportunity to ask him questions about what I feel and why I feel it when I am practicing.

His answers were sage.

Murray used to live in Central New York State. He has done many things and lived in different places in our area. About twenty years ago, he owned a horse farm in Hamilton, NY.

Knowing I had to leave to teach a yoga class, he asked me if I had time to listen to one story.

"Yes," I said.

Gently in a quiet voice, he recounted this story—

One day, a man called him and asked him if he had a horse farm and stables and if it was located on many acres adjacent to Lake Moraine. Murray replied, "Yes I do." The voice on the other end told him that if he would have four or five of his best horses ready for riding in the barn and free up his day, the other horses and his riding stable would be well cared for. He was asked to not to ask questions or share this phone call with anyone. Murray agreed. He thought, "Someone else was going to care for the other fifteen horses and do his daily work and all he had to do was lead a ride, why not?"

At the appointed time, a car drove up to the barn. Out stepped what he described as "some unusual-looking" men. He thought to himself, "Ok so they look different."

After greetings, they mounted the horses and rode for about five hours over his land into state land and back again. During that time, one of the unusual looking men on horseback, told Murray that he used to ride yak, camels and horses and that it was a long time since he had such an opportunity to ride the land like they were doing. He was very much enjoying being on horseback.

When they arrived back at the barn, they dismounted. The unusual man grateful for the ride came over to Murray. He placed his hands on Murray's shoulders dispensing a special blessing.

Murray told me his life has not been the same since that moment.

That man was the Dalai Lama who was being harbored at Colgate University.

As Murray was telling me this story, I watched him stand up, come over to me and put his hands on my shoulders. He then transferred to me the same blessing as he received from the Dalai Lama. His eyes were full of tears, his emotion was profound. He said, "you will make a difference."

Imagine how easy it was to drive home after that!

Life is full of miracles when you least expect them. For a few years, I have been the first one in line at the "no tickets available" line to see the Dalai Lama—both at Colgate and Cornell Universities. Who would have guessed that he would come to me at my friend Martha's house out on a country road in the form of a seventy-plus year old stranger?

Pink Flannel

A pink flannel shirt has hung in my closet for more than twenty years.

We have two seasons in Central New York— summer and winter. Twice a year, I clean and sort through my wardrobe in anticipation of each season. Out-of-season clothing is carried to the cedar closet in the basement. Clothing seldom or never worn is delegated to the give-away bag. Some items go out of style. Each season, I might add one or two trendy items to brighten my spirits. Such additions seldom stay around for long. Some articles are symptoms of impulse buying. It may have been a bad day. A few things no longer fit well. With age and contentment, I added more of me. As for the pink flannel shirt—it is not today's fashion. It was not an impulse buy. It fits, if a little more snugly.

The store I purchased it at was a respected retailer— Sibley's, a store no longer in existence. Sibley's was bought-out by Kauffmann's. Kauffmann's was bought-out by Macy's. With each conglomerate buy-out, the racks have become more jumbled.

I liked shopping at Sibley's. It smelled sweet and clean like fine stores do. The racks and kiosks were orderly, the lighting pleasant, the clothing displayed in a way to enhance its attractiveness. The fabrics felt rich. My flannel shirt embodies all of this, and more.

It was its color that first caught my eye—a gentle pink. I felt the fabric for its tight weave good for warmth, its softness soothing. Slipping it over my shoulders I felt feminine. I liked the glow it gave my face as I looked into the mirror. The pink and white plaid made me feel vibrant. I handed over my credit card. The clerk carefully folded the shirt, wrapped it in tissue, gently placed it in a sturdy white shopping bag with a handle.

I wore this shirt in winter when the sky was heavy and gray, when snow fell and piled up against the house, when ice etched the corners of the windows, when breath froze outside in tiny crystals.

Twenty-some years ago in March when winter stubbornly hung on, I wore that shirt to a hospital where they cut through my breast to see what I was holding there.

I was forty years old. My birthday was in February. I spent every day of that month worrying. Each night, as I lay in bed with the stillness of that season holding its breath over my home, I put my fingers to my breast to feel the lump that grew just beneath the surface of my flesh. In the morning, I checked to see if it was still there. Twenty-eight days, I anticipated, worried, fretted, agonized, dwelled on and tortured myself over the errant cells that made up the knot of tissue dictating my fate. I was haunted by decisions of radiation and chemotherapy, of relinquishing any control I alluded to having over my life. I struggled with surrendering to strangers who would cut through my flesh, wipe clean the blood that oozed free, stitch my skin back together and then tell me what they found.

I was in queue. There was no hurrying time. Other women were ahead of me. The surgeon only did breast biopsies on Tuesdays. I waited, talked with God, took long walks, watched it snow. When the appointed time arrived, I put on my pink flannel shirt. At the hospital, I was more than reluctant to trade it for a flimsy, rough, open-along-the back hospital gown. With the care of unwrapping a delicate gift, I slipped the shirt from my shoulders, folded it lovingly, placed it in an industrial gray numbered bin allotted for my personal belongings—jeans, underwear, socks, sneakers and the pink flannel shirt.

I was awake during the surgery. The physician ordered someone to run the excised tissue sample to the lab as I lay on the table awaiting the next step—more surgery or stitch and go. The phone rang in the operating room. The surgeon spoke with the pathologist. Good news. The lump that looked like a tiny yellowish brain of convoluted tissue had a name—fibroadenoma, a benign tumor.

When it was time to go home, I remember the luxury of placing the pink flannel back onto my shoulders, gliding my arms through its sleeves, feeling the tenderness of soft cotton over my non bandaged breast.

Today, that fabric is thinner having tumbled through many launderings. It is clean and pressed, and though I never wear it, it remains in my closet.

I could put it in the give-away bag that I take to the Opportunity Shop about once a month. But I don't. I could use it for a polishing cloth, but I can't take scissors to it. I could make a quilt using the flannel for some of the squares. I don't have the heart to take it apart. It would be good to give it to someone in need of a pink flannel shirt to keep warm and feel pretty. I could frame it as a wall hanging. I could even make it into a doll for a little girl. Certainly, there are dozens of uses for this shirt I no longer wear that continues to hang in my closet.

Each time I touch the pink flannel, it speaks to me of gratitude, mortality, life, hope, the mystery of why some of us squeak through the tough times, while others endure more suffering, pass from earth. Sometimes, when I am going through my closet, I fondle the fabric. I take in the "pink of it." I remember the moment of good news. It's not easy to let go of good news.

In the Light

Eeeeeeeeeeerrrreeeeeeeeeeech! Steel wheels came to a halt in the Frankfurt railroad station. We were on our way north from Switzerland. We had been traveling for almost six weeks bearing backpacks and sleeping in small inns and hostels in England, France, Spain, Italy and Greece. Many nights we slept on the train. With a student Eurrail pass in hand, we had unlimited use of mainland Europe's rails. Sleeping on the train saved on hotel fare while we were transported to our next destination. We had no agenda, no schedule. Like nomads, we moved from city to city on a whim of romance, chasing art galleries, monuments, relatives and seashores.

Laura had cramps that morning and did not want to leave the train. We had about a half hour stopover to let off and take on more passengers.

I said, "We don't have any Deustch marks. If we want food, we won't have the right currency to buy some. How about if you stay here with our stuff and I go change some money?"

"Okay, thanks Raine," she said.

I left Laura in our compartment slouched in a corner surrounded by our belongings, while I disembarked. I walked through the station amidst the sounds of trains and people echoing in the girded high arched steel ceilings. I entered the terminal only to exit briefly onto a busy street where I spied a bank. The teller was quick and efficient as I exchanged a few dollars. It took me only a matter of minutes, but when I returned to the track where I left Laura and our train, both had vanished. I looked up at the rail track number. It looked like the same one I had left behind. I looked through the station. Trains in Germany were on a precise schedule. Did I get it wrong? No, this was where I had left my friend, our transportation, accommodations and worldly goods. I was stunned, paralyzed. The track was empty. Laura was gone as were my passport, address book, maps, guidebooks, clothes, toiletries and remaining American Travelers Checks. We had no set itinerary. Cell phones were a thing of the future. How would we find each other?

I stood, my mind working at lightning speed wondering whether to take a train to the next destination on the schedule. But what direction would I go? Would it be best to remain here? My hope was that Laura would either be waiting for me or come back for me. I saw a train slowly heading for our track. As it began to loom larger in my sight, I saw a small round head pushing its way out of the window— its crop of short brown hair being rustled by the breeze of the of the moving train. I was working this out in my mind when I saw that a hand was eagerly waving. And then I saw the smile, that broad white familiar smile. It was Laura. As soon as I safely could, I jumped aboard. We hugged. We were ecstatic to see each other. She explained that the train had left to add more cars, but she didn't know it at the time and was worried about leaving me in Frankfurt.

I sat at my desk remembering this story Monday, June 14, 2004. Earlier that morning I was sorting through my business mail and smelled the fragrance of roses. I thought to myself, I wish they would stop sending perfume samples through the mail. I sifted through the envelopes but none bore a scent. I rifled through the magazines, but none carried the perfume. I pulled my clothes close to my nose thinking they had rested near a sachet. But the bouquet did not come from what I was wearing. I walked into my bookkeeper's office, but there were no roses there. I walked into the hall. There was no trail of roses there. The heady scent was becoming stronger and it seemed to be around me. I said, "this is crazy."

I thought to call a friend who is clairvoyant. Luckily, he was available.

"You don't happen to know why I'm smelling the scent of roses this morning would you?"

"Yes, someone is by you, your friend."

"Are you sure it is my friend."

"She has a short white top on with kind of flared sleeves, sort of like an angel would wear, but not an angel. I don't know what they call those sleeves. And she has short light pink pants on. Short pants."

"Capris?"

"Yes, and there is light on her head and…her feet, her feet are not on the earth. She is over the burden. And she is waving and smiling. Nice. Real nice. I… rene, I—rene."

"Irene? Who is Irene?"

"I am so bad with names," he said. "I—rene. She's waving."

"Laura?" I asked. "My friend's name is Laura."

"No, she is saying Irene and waving. She is waving good-bye now. She said she won't be back for awhile. She blew you a kiss. It is blue, very spiritual. There is spirituality coming from her fingertips. She is uplifted, light, smiling..."

The evening before this morning, Laura's husband called me to tell me of Laura's passing. She had been battling a recurrence of cancer that had begun in her breast and aggressively spread throughout her body. It was hard to believe we had just danced at her son's wedding less than three month's ago. She had looked perfect. We had held on to each other, laughing, kicking up our heels to her favorite Motown music. We were a tight group of five who graduated together and remained friends for more than three decades. Now Laura was gone.

She left and the scent of roses faded.

"Who is Irene?" I wanted to know. I searched the internet. The name Irene, I learned, means peace.
I thought about emailing the other girls. I was reluctant. They were grieving, too.

"Plus," I thought to myself," who is going to believe this story?"

Still the image seemed meant to share. It was Mary who grew up with Laura in Brookyln who simply replied, "Not Irene. Hi Raine!" She was calling me by my nickname.

Suddenly, I felt like I was in Frankfurt seeing a train arrive with a small round head pushing its way out of the window, sun lighting its crop of short brown hair tousled by the onward motion of the train, a hand reaching out eagerly waving.

"Hi Raine."

Whether I wait here or "board the train" to the next destination, Laura gave me a gift. She reminded me that we will meet again.

My Greatest Teachers

My eyes were fixed on the road as I was driving. My mother was in the passenger's seat next to me looking sadly out the window. She knew more of what was about to happen than I did that day. She took the moment to look straight ahead and say, "Raine, you have been the love of my life." I was struck silent for in those words was something besides what she felt for me throughout our life together. In those words, she was expressing her love and saying good-bye at the same time. I did not want to hear the good-bye. I looked over at my mother briefly and drove a little faster.

We were on our way to a doctor's appointment to find out why my mother wasn't feeling well.

My youngest brother the baby of the family, passed away the previous year. After that, a light in my mother went dim. Her mourning was so deep that she put aside her will to live. We were learning that emotions often have a profound effect on the body.

No one ever wants to hear the news we took home with us that afternoon. The ride back to her house was somber I don't remember what we said. News like that can dull a memory. I do know that we were given an appointment with a specialist and we would go forward.

In the days that ensued, my mother digested the news. She looked around at her life, her children, her grandchildren, her sister and something changed inside her. She decided in the face of dying, she wanted to live. I was bound and determined to help her any way I could toward that goal we shared. I thought if we did everything we could, if we prayed hard, if we had the right practitioners, if we worked at nursing and nurturing, we could have more time.

For the next two months, daily life became a dizzying whirlwind as we were constantly in crisis mode. Mom suffered a stroke losing her ability to speak. There were blood clots to address. Surgery. Ambulance rides to the hospital. Comfort care rides home and to a nursing facility. After the first stroke, she came to our house so that we could care for her there. She was never in any one of these places very long before another crisis erupted. Care for her was intensive and seemingly always immediate.

Our daughters were quick to volunteer. They arranged their time so that our youngest Ariana would take nights caring for her grandmother at the hospital and I could be there during daytime to talk with doctors. Our eldest Elise would come on weekends from Connecticut to help with her grandmother and give Ariana respite. My mother's only remaining sister came to sit with Mom too, my brother and his family brought food and presence, my husband helped often taking our daughters to dinner to give them a sense of normality away from the hospital, nieces and nephews offered support. They all came to show their love for the woman who they knew as strong with a sense of humor, who was down-to-earth, matter-of-fact and wise, who above all loved each of us unconditionally and was never afraid to show it. Loving care was the only gift we all had left to give back to her—mother, grandmother, sister and aunt—who had given us the gift of time with her whole heart. We surrounded her with love hoping beyond hope to take her home.

At the end of those two months, we did take her home, but it was to make her comfortable to live out her remaining time. The night she was ready to transition to another life, we stood around her bed to say our good-byes. She was awake. She looked intently and somewhat puzzled at us and then in between where each of us was standing and then her eyes returned to me. There were others around her bedside only she could see. She left peacefully washed in the soft tears of her immediate family.

In the end, it was she who gave us the greatest of gifts. In our caring for her, she gave my daughters and me a bond between us far too strong to ever be broken.

Ariana and I were cleaning mom's bedroom the following afternoon. It was a warm and pleasant day for November. A window was open to let in fresh air and sunlight. I paused to look outside at the schoolyard across the street. Children were laughing and playing. My grief was heavy. I missed my mother.

I said to Ariana, "Don't you wish this was just a normal day, that you were out playing like those kids?"

She replied, "No Mom, I'm sure there have been plenty of kids who wished they had had a grandmother like mine."

Penny for Your Dream

Not long after my mother passed away, she came to me.

Was it a dream or a visit?

My mother had been seriously ill for two months. She subsequently suffered a stroke and could not speak. My two twenty-something year-old daughters and I cared for her. The girls took turns tending to her during the night, while I was by her side during the day.

The morning after she passed, I was gazing through the open window of her bedroom at the school across the street listening to children playing during recess.

My mother had lost both her parents by the time she was eighteen. I was born when she was twenty-three. Mothering came naturally to her. She was a nurturer mixing fun, discipline and creativity in rearing her children. Through our years together, she called me by name, but she often called me Sis, too. We were mother and daughter yet, often we were like sisters sharing laughter and sadness. Other times we were like friends supporting each other working out problems.

After my father passed on, Mom and I spent more and more time together. I called her every morning before I left for work. She often came to the office for a short visit telling me about the pennies she found on her walk. "Why do kids just throw them away like they have no value?" she asked indignantly.

She feared thunderstorms, having been struck by lightning when she was a child. Those nights of predicted storms she would arrive at our house carrying a paper grocery bag with her nightgown, toothbrush, face cream and a hairbrush. She did not want to be alone. Our eldest was away at college, so Mom slept in her room.

One night, after Mom passed away, I was startled from a dream so real that I believed my mother was present.

She appeared glowing white in an exquisite white

nightgown standing by my side of the bed. Her face was serious. I said, "Mom, what's the matter? Is everything all right? Is there a thunderstorm?"

She did not reply. She just looked deeply into my eyes. She did not speak during her final days on earth and she did not speak now. She disappeared as I came into full wakefulness and went racing through the house to find her, but she was not in any of our rooms. I so longed to talk to her.

I could not go back to sleep, The dream was so vivid, my heart was racing. I looked for her to return.

A few days after that dream, my husband received challenging news. I believe my mother came to me the night she did to warn me, to let me know she was by my side, that we would come through it. And we did.

A few years later, she visited again in a dream, but this time it was not an image. It was a knowing, a sense of her presence, again with a seriousness I couldn't shake.

A challenge with another family member arose. I finally said, "Mom, thank you for alerting me when life is going to get a little rocky, but could you please come and bring good news, too? "

Now she leaves pennies in unexpected places to show she's thinking of us.

Message from Michael

A few years ago, I received a surprising gift. It was a book written by a woman who communicated with angels. It was sent to me from a friend—a marine turned cop turned prosecutor in one of the nation's largest cities. The prosecutor and I worked together on the board of a real estate association. We had never shared a conversation about angels.

The book was an easy, enjoyable read. When I finished reading it, I felt the need to send it to my daughter who lives in New York City.

On a rainy Thursday afternoon, shortly after I had sent the book out to my daughter and after she had read it, I was at an appointment with my acupuncturist. My left knee was the problem. It was inflamed and nothing seemed to be helping alleviate the discomfort. X rays showed no muscular or skeletal issues.

My acupuncturist uses a specialized protocol to help relieve her patients' intolerances due to food, environmental and emotional causes. She treated me for an allergy to grain/gluten. As we were completing our visit, she told me that I should get my thyroid checked and that I should drink more water. I thought it curious that she would give me that advice, as we had not discussed anything to do with my thyroid or hydration. Her words to me seemed almost an afterthought.

I said I would try to drink more and that I would look into getting my thyroid checked. It's always been hard for me to hydrate through the day. I am not often thirsty. I have to consciously work at remembering to take in fluids. I also didn't have a doctor to call on at the time. I might have let her counsel slide if not for a phone call a few minutes later.

As I was about to leave the office, I gave my acupuncturist the prayer from the Archangel Michael that appeared in the book about the woman and angels with whom she communicated. My acupuncturist is a friend and very spiritual person. She was grateful for the small rectangle of paper I handed her with the words of the prayer I had handwritten on it.

No sooner had I climbed into my car to drive home than my cell phone rang. I was still in the office-building parking lot, the car not yet started. It was cool and damp in my vehicle. I answered the phone when I saw it was my daughter calling from Manhattan.

"Mom, I am having the weirdest day!" she exclaimed.

"How so?" I asked.

"A friend and I decided to have a cultural day. We were at the Metropolitan Museum of Art when my friend said her feet hurt so much she had to leave at that very moment. I said to her, 'right now?' She told me she couldn't stay an extra minute. And because her feet hurt, we decided to take a cab. I had some errands to run, so she left me off between 61st and 62nd Streets at Broadway. It felt like I no sooner got out of the cab than this woman came out of nowhere and was in my face. She said she had information for me.

"I told her I didn't have any money for her," my daughter explained.

"What did she want? Did she look crazy?" I questioned.

"No, she was just regular looking. She looked like she could be a mom from New Jersey. She looked Native American and she was wearing a Cartier watch."

"Did she want money?" I asked.

"She said, it was alright that I didn't have money for her. She said she had a message for me from the Archangel Michael."

Complete silence now filled the space between my daughter and me.

"Mom, are you there?" my daughter asked in frustration.

"Yes, I'm here. I'm listening," I replied.

"She said the Archangel Michael told her to tell me to get my thyroid checked and to drink more water. I said, my thyroid? Are you sure? I don't feel like my thyroid is a problem. She said, well it could be me or someone close to me.

"Mom! Are you laughing? Why are you laughing?

I'm serious," my daughter shot back to me in frustration.

"I know you're serious," I said gathering my composure. "I'm laughing because I just left my acupuncturist. She just told me to have my thyroid checked and to drink more water. Also, I gave her the prayer from the Archangel Michael from that book I sent you."

"Oh," she quietly replied.

My daughter was having her conversation with the Native American woman in Manhattan at the same time my acupuncturist and I were talking about MY thyroid, MY drinking more water and the Archangel Michael.

We marveled over the synchronicity of this event, this miracle that occurred over a distance of two hundred seventy miles.

In getting my thyroid checked, I discovered that my body was having a problem processing cheese and grain. Those items created mucous in my system that was affecting my left knee. When I eliminated those items from my diet, the heat and swelling in my knee disappeared. As for my thyroid—it indeed was sluggish. Supplements to my daily regimen helped it to healthy functioning.

Thank you, Archangel Michael!

Paths Not on the Map

Sometimes we are guided down paths we didn't even know were there.

During the 1990s, I experienced several losses of family members and friends and a great deal of stress on several fronts. My father passed on suddenly. I inherited his work of carrying on our family business. My husband was deeply immersed in building our real estate brokerage. Our daughters were teenagers, one of whom was readying to go off to college and my mother needed my support for this new chapter of her life—living alone.

Trying to fit everything into a shrinking clock and making sure each family member's needs were met, had impact on my immune system. I found myself making a career of doctors' appointments that were addressing symptoms but were not dealing with the cause of my health issues. It felt like I was in a downward spiral.

One morning, I saw a blurb in the local newspaper about a meditation class at the local Zen Center, a place unfamiliar to me. Somehow, I knew in my gut this was something I needed to do. I enrolled in a six-week session.

As I moved into the practice of meditation week after week, I was surprised to find dealing with my daily responsibilities easier to handle. I discovered a center of calm and peace within myself. When the chaos of busy lives enveloped me, I remained undisturbed.

I was so encouraged by these results that I stepped a little further out of my comfort zone and found a yoga class. I didn't know anything about yoga, but it seemed like a logical next step. Yoga classes were not popular in our area at that time. I persevered in finding opportunities. I became a yoga nomad moving from one session that ended to the next one that began. One was held in a college cafeteria, another in a dance school, yet another in a women's wellness center. I was becoming stronger, healthier, and happier to the point it was noticeable to others. And my medical tests improved at each appointment.

Every morning as I walked by a vacant store front

in the building where I worked, I thought to myself, "this would make a good yoga studio." I wanted to share with others what I had received in my practice—greater vitality.

I hired a teacher and convinced a group of women to enroll in classes. The teacher was very good, but after several weeks, she wanted to spend more time with a new grandchild. I hired another teacher. She also was good, but after several weeks, she decided she didn't want to come out in the evening to teach. She had already put in a full day at her regular job. I hired a third teacher. After the third class, she didn't show up. She had her own business to run.

There I sat facing a class of women looking at me waiting to practice yoga. They asked me to teach the class.

I was a novice at yoga. I had no training and didn't feel knowledgeable enough to instruct others. They encouraged me to teach them what I knew. So I did and they showed up week after week for class.

I discovered a ninety-hour Yoga for Health training class fifteen minutes from my home. This allowed me to learn more and yet have time to take care of my responsibilities. At the end of the training, the instructor told us that our successful completion of this program did not satisfy Yoga Alliance's requirements for certification. It was disappointing, but I felt it gave me a good background for the next step. I searched for a 200-hour Yoga Alliance sanctioned teacher training. They all seemed so far away.

A friend insisted I apply to a program less than two hours from home.

My first training was in the Kripalu style of Hatha yoga. My worry now was how I would keep up with or fit in with an alignment-based Iyengar style of yoga in a class of twenty-one students most likely younger than I. I was fifty-eight.

The program was more than teaching poses and breath work. It included study in philosophy, anatomy, and Ayurveda (the health science of yoga.) My interest was in helping others to heal as I had healed. My friend continued to prod me to apply for the program. I had so much on my plate at the time, but I sent in my application.

It was a grueling challenge of balancing family, maintaining our business, teaching my yoga class and traveling the interstate once a week plus one or two weekends a month for six months.

I was accepted into the program.

My mother passed away less than two months before I began that teacher training program.

I believe now that I would have drowned in grief without entering into Open Sky Yoga's Essential Teacher Training.

It was hard work. It was learning a new language along with poses and technique. Sometimes, it was overwhelming, yet at the same time, I was fascinated by what I was studying.

At graduation in June, I sat in the closing circle amidst rose petals, tears, and new friends/fellow teachers. I knew in my heart I had heeded a call. And I also knew that by having stepped out of my comfort zone, I became stronger not only physically, but emotionally and spiritually for meeting a challenge I doubted myself for taking on.

I had no ambitions in my earlier life to be a yoga teacher. It couldn't have been further from my mind, but at each turn of events, I was guided down a path I hadn't foreseen. I am in my seventies now and still teaching.

Avatar

I was leaving the next day for Toronto when my cousin asked,

"You are going all that way for only one night?"

"Yes"

"Why"

"To receive darshan from Amma"

"What is darshan?"

"Well, it's a blessing."

"Who is Amma?"

"Amma is an avatar, a living saint from India."

"An avatar? A human one, not like the movie?"

"Yes"

"What do you get for that?" I had to think about this.

"Well, you like walking in nature, right?"

"Yes"

"How would you explain what you get from that?"

She considered my question. Understanding was beginning to seep in.

"For me, visiting Amma is like that. It is a sense of peace, the essence of being cleansed from the outside noise of the world. There isn't something material, maybe not even tangible that I can explain to you. It is a joyful experience. I suppose it's like going to a party for the soul."

A Favor?

As I ended the call with my friend, I felt my anxiety rising. The favor she asked of me was one I had never done for anyone before. And I had agreed to do it without talking with my husband about it first. I would be opening our home to an unknown male with a questionable reputation. My friend asked me to house him for a night or two until she could make time for the three-and -a-half-hour drive from her home to mine to meet and retrieve him.

Rocky arrived one late afternoon in December 2008.

On his arrival for the layover with us, he trotted down the transport's ramp aiming for me by the side of the driveway, stood up and gave me a kiss like we had been waiting for each other all our lives. He presented with a troubling hole in his side, a "gift" from a Pitbull's teeth at one of his previous foster homes.

Rocky paid little mind to me after that kiss as he walked over the threshold into our house going straight for a drink. I had put some food out for him, but he decided to explore the whole house first as I followed behind him with trepidation.

He was dark and handsome. It didn't take long for me to assess his intelligence. He ranked at the top of the class. Rocky was a rescue dog, part German Shepherd, part Rottweiler.

He proved to be a good guest.

My friend came as she said she would taking Rocky back to her house. I missed him terribly. We had made a profound connection that I didn't immediately understand in the two days we were together.

Rocky lasted a week at my friend's home. There were two other dogs and two cats in his new household. His prospective owner felt Rocky was not fitting in and causing anxiety with the other pets. She decided to return him to the rescue organization.

I wanted him, but it was Christmas in two days. Our home fills with people for the holiday especially Christmas Eve when we host a large open house party for family and friends. There is a great deal of food and commotion to add to the festivities.

My friend and I arranged that if she could keep him until the day after Christmas, I would meet her halfway and retrieve Rocky from her eventually arranging to adopt him. She happily agreed to this.

When Rocky's rescuer heard of our plans, she didn't want to take any chances with leaving the dog where he might cause a situation. She liked the idea of my adopting him, but not the delay in bringing him into my home. She brightened when she heard the name of the city where my friend and I were to meet. She said, "my sister lives there and she will be passing right by your Thruway exit on the way to my home on Christmas Eve."

"Christmas Eve?" I thought, as my heart sank. Life was going to be difficult for a few days.

And so it was, on Christmas Eve, I left my kitchen and met the rescuer's sister at the appointed time and exit. Rocky happily leapt from her car into mine. He was going to celebrate Christmas with us.

We were met with a stony welcome at home. "What are you thinking bringing a new dog here that we know nothing about when we're expecting over twenty people and it's Christmas Eve!!!!"

I was a wreck. It was such an emotional time.

We finally settled into our duties readying for company when I was called into the dining room momentarily for a decision on platter placement. When I returned to the kitchen, I found that slices of Italian specialty salamis I had been arranging were wiped clean. Rocky so quietly and stealthily had made those slices his own.

Our daughter and her Labrador Retriever, Beans arrived at the house. It was decided that Rocky and Beans would take turns being at the party. When it was Rocky's turn to come downstairs, I held him on leash. I was distracted introducing him to our family and friends. In one swipe of the tongue, he ate a whole wedge of Brie from where it was displayed on the coffee table. At least our guests thought it was funny.

We made it through the night without further incident. Christmas morning, we sat in the sunroom around the tree to open presents. There was a new collar and leash for Beans from me. As our daughter opened the gift and held it in her hands, she looked from it to Rocky seeing a need. She reached out and offered it back to me for Rocky, his very first and only gift that Christmas.

His adoption papers arrived on the Epiphany, January 6. I signed them immediately mailing them back to the rescue organization the same day.

In the weeks to follow, I brought him with me to my yoga studio and office. He proved to be a gentleman and a morale booster. He went to work with me every day. He was too intelligent to stay home alone all day. He had a bed in my office and many friends in and around the building. He took joy in visiting tenants garnering snacks from their desk drawers or their restaurants. He looked forward to going everywhere with me. Anytime, I went toward the door, he was on all paws ready to go.

With each day, I could feel another chamber of my heart open that had been locked. He made us laugh, he comforted us, shared our grief and our celebrations. He loved his family, was excited when they returned home after long absences at school or at their homes away from home.

He became my best friend, a patient traveler, a food devotee, a guarder of the kitchen (known to burgle at times,) an eager co-pilot of hikes and adventures, a most quiet and steadfast companion. Most of all Rocky was a teacher, a teacher of unconditional love.

Watch Dog

In the evening when the windows of our house were dark with winter on the other side of them and I was home alone, Zoe barked at me.

Zoe was our thirteen-year-old sable-colored Sheltie. She was prim and proper for a dog, rather regal in the way she carried herself. She didn't tolerate getting dirty or the puppy antics of our daughter's chocolate Labrador.

Years earlier, when we went to adopt a puppy, it was Zoe who chose us. We stood in the breeder's outdoor pen among her litter surveying the puppies, watching their behavior, trying to make our decision. One of our children campaigned for an active energetic male puppy that was running in circles around her. He seemed a handful. It was Zoe, who with a sense of calm and knowing, came to stand at our feet with her eyes lifted to mine, asked if our choice could be her.

Zoe was the puppy who came home with us. She was a happy bundle of fur with a little potbelly. She was easy to train. She caught on quickly to whatever we asked of her. She learned to love chasing a soccer ball much to the chagrin of our daughters who were practicing making goals. When she was restrained from the game, she barked and barked. We often had to put her in the house because of her interference. Still, from inside the sliding glass door, she watched the action out-of-doors and barked and barked. When anyone jumped into the lake from our dock, she barked and barked. When the UPS man came to the door, Zoe barked. In fact, Zoe often tried to "talk" to us when she wanted something. I thought I had learned her signals well.

I still had more to learn.

One evening near Christmas, years later, we were home alone, just Zoe and me. In northeast United States, it is seasonally dark and cold then. The house was unusually quiet. Television wasn't on. I was reading. Zoe was peering down an unlit hallway. She began barking and barking at me. She barked incessantly. I opened the door for her to go out, but she did not want to go out. I offered her a treat, but she didn't want that either. I pet her, yet she continued to bark. Because of her age, I questioned whether she was slowly becoming senile. I couldn't pacify her. Because of the dark and quiet enveloping us, I began to feel unsettled. The barking only stopped when Joel came home. This happened several times.

Out of desperation, I decided to consult an animal communicator who had helped found a nearby animal sanctuary. I didn't know what to expect.

This is what she told me. There is a man who comes to see you. He especially likes to come near holidays. He's holding a ball. He comes to check up on his son and watches over your house.

Tears streamed down my cheeks.

I had lost my younger brother Bill a few months before to sudden illness. He reluctantly left a nine-year old son.

Funny, how things work. Bill was the one who introduced me to my husband, Joel. Joel had been one of Bill's high school teachers. My brother often came home with stories of things that happened in Joel's class. When Bill was president of Student Council his senior year, he asked me to chaperone a Friday night dance. Joel was also a chaperone. In time, Bill was a groom's men in our wedding. We were godparents to his son.

Bill brought Brady to us often, first in infant blankets then on walking adventures through fields when the boy was older. We hosted Brady's birthday celebrations with our extended family. Looking back, Bill had taken great care to create a bond between us and his son almost as if he knew something about the future.

When Bill passed on, we embraced Brady as one of our own children. Brady's mom was generous in letting us share their son one day during the week and every other weekend until Brady's class work and activities became more demanding of his time. He often went on vacation with us.

When the animal communicator gave me her message, I knew in an instant that my brother was the image Zoe was barking at. He was smart to carry a ball to get

Zoe's attention. He knew she would bark. From then on when Zoe looked down the hall when there seemed to be no one there, I knew who was there and it was comforting to know he was watching over us.

Michael at the Crossing

On a visit to New York State's Adirondacks, we took the opportunity to visit the house where my husband's grandparents had lived. The reason for our visit to the old homestead was two-fold—to remember times past and to enjoy a lovely family birthday dinner.

The house was no longer a home. Both grandparents passed away many years ago and after decades of residential owners, the house was converted to a restaurant.

There are framed black and white photos of the owners' family all along the walls. It felt good seeing that a family is honored there.

We introduced ourselves to the hostess who in turn introduced us to the owner/chef. She was delighted to meet us and hear stories about the house back when Joel's grandparents lived there.

The conversation moved from the exchange of family stories to intriguing after she inquired, "Did someone die here? And was someone, Michael? We've heard that name."

We were all stunned. My husband dug deep trying to recollect a story about a Michael. Our children looked on wondering, too.

We couldn't recall one reference. So, we left it where it was, a question.

It just so happened that we were visiting with family the next day and posed the question to my husband's brother Phil.

It turns out on February 3rd, 1963, Phil's and Joel's grandfather had come home from shoveling roofs. He called upstairs from the pantry to ask Joel's grandmother if she wanted coffee. When she came downstairs to the pantry, she found that her husband had passed away on the pantry floor.

Phil told us Michael was brother to their grandfather.

We later shared this with the chef/owner. She replied, "Sometimes when I get in [the restaurant] in the morning, there will be a coffee mug upside down on the floor in the pantry."

For Salt of the Earth Bistro

91

Earth School

They say earth is a school and for a soul to advance in its spiritual journey, the soul makes a contract with Source/God and incarnates on this planet. It is also said that this is the most challenging of spiritual schools.

We decide with whom we share our earthly lives and what challenges we will work to meet. It's all decided by each of us before we arrive. Somehow when we fight our way through the birth canal and take that first searing breath, we forget all about that contract and become totally immersed in the human drama. We are spiritual beings having a human experience with feelings and foibles.

Those who choose the most humbling and difficult circumstances either are satisfying Karma or advancing far more quickly than the most ordinary of us.

I have no doubt that Bill was on a spiritual journey, that those of us who share our lives here are from the same soul pod, that we chose to be with each other here and that we will be together again.

When I took my first Reiki training and was immersed in the ceremony of attunement, Bill was there. His presence startled me. I had never had such an experience. I didn't see him, I didn't hear him, but I absolutely felt his presence as tears rose in my eyes and gently coursed down my cheeks.

When Zoe, our sheltie who has since also passed from this incarnation, and I were in the house alone at night just before a holiday, she would unnerve me. She would bark and bark at me, then look down the hallway and then at me. She wouldn't stop. She didn't have to go out. She wasn't hungry. She wasn't in pain, but the barking continued. When Joel or the girls came home, the barking stopped. It freaked me out enough for me to contact an animal communicator. The communicator told me thins: "a man comes to your house. He is carrying a ball. He comes to check on his son and see what's happening. He especially likes to come at holiday time when everyone is together. "It was Bill. (Zoe loved chasing a soccer ball. That's how he captured her attention and therefore mine.)

Recently, a yoga student who is also an empath offered the information that my brother likes to be near me, he likes to be with me in quiet times when I am alone. She said, he is sorry for leaving so suddenly and for leaving work undone.

I have sensed enough confirmation to accept this and am honored to enjoy this gift. I think he is probably working very hard to help me "see."

Just after Bill passed from this incarnation, his nine-year-old son asked me to read the Book of Revelations from the Bible to see if we could find where his dad might have gone.

It was a dark time. It was hard to find Bill then. It was hard to find ourselves in all the pain of loss. Now, I am absolutely convinced he is not far at all from us. We have eyeglasses to see far, eyeglasses to see near, goggles to see through the dark, some to see underwater. If only we had some kind of eyewear that would help us see past the veil. Until then, I am content to feel his loving presence.

Precious Human Birth

Some years ago, I was invited to a yoga workshop at Open Sky Yoga Center in Rochester, NY where I studied yoga teacher training with Francois Raoult.

After the workshop, Francois invited a few of us to dinner at his house. It's always fun to have dinner at Francois'. He is a creative cook, musician and artist.

I was surprised to see his dining room completely taken over by Sampa, a Tibetan refugee and woodcarver. Some of Sampa's completed work was on a table in the foyer.

I was drawn like a magnet to a carving, a turtle with a ring around his neck and a series of Buddhist symbols surrounding it. I had no idea of its meaning or what was soon to transpire.

Try as I might to be distracted, I just couldn't get that carving out of my mind.

I first inquired of Sampa in an email, but his English was limited, so Francois became the broker. The cost of the carving was more than I felt comfortable spending. I turned to other things, still the thought of it wouldn't go away. There is life in Sampa's work.

Emails sailed back and forth, and as you might guess, I was soon to be the owner of the carving. Francois insisted on sending it out right away and would trust me to bring the cash the next time I was in Rochester. I wasn't going to make that trip any time soon, yet I didn't want a debt hanging over my head. I had to figure out a way to get payment to him.

I counted out the agreed upon bills and placed them neatly in a paperback book, wrapped it carefully and mailed it to Francois.

He brought it to my attention a few days later that my email to him saying the carving arrived to me and his email to me saying the book arrived to him were six seconds apart.

In a later email, Francois wrote: Sampa "wants me to tell you he sent all the money to his mother in Lhasa, Tibet. He never gave money to his mother before and felt very good. It was hard to transfer to China as Western

Union does not exist there. His mother took one month by horse to arrive to Lhasa and will do a pilgrimage. Be blessed, really."

The title of the carving is "Precious Human Birth." It took Sampa a month to fabricate it.

The story is from the Buddha in the Chiggala Sutta—

Imagine there is a turtle adrift at sea that only surfaces every 100 years.
Now imagine there is a small ring in this vast sea.
It is more likely for the turtle to accidentally poke its head through that ring than to be born a human being.
Treasure the good work you can do with your life!

Postscript: I learned later that among Sampa's work is an altar he made for the Dalai Lama.

PART III

Living Among Life

The greatest act of human courage isn't climbing mountains,
conquering countries, or fighting in wars; it is walking into
the mysterious abyss of one's own inner self and truthfully
face one's own pain and tortured Shadows.

~Lonerwolf

Living and Accepting Without Judgment

I have an acquaintance who found me on Facebook after reading a story I wrote for *Chicken Soup for the Soul.* I have never met him, but we have become friends through correspondence. He lives far from me in the Middle East.

One day he sent me a photo of a beautiful young girl. It was his daughter.

We talked about daughters and how they are ours for all our life. You know that poem? "A son is yours until he takes a wife, but a daughter is yours for all your life." My friend wrote to me about his family's losses. Because of his wife's gestational diabetes, they lost three babies, two daughters and a son. The daughter they have is all the more precious.

Another friend called me to deliver a message. Conversations have a way of branching off in many directions. This one included the abuse she experienced in childhood. It is always heart-wrenching to hear such stories. They are often more common than we want to believe.

Grief can be so overwhelming. The longer we live, the more we experience it—being loved and loving when it may not be returned in the same way as we offer it, rearing children whose paths diverge from our own direction and compass, parents and step parents, siblings, aunts, uncles and friends who may betray us.

All are circumstances of living on Earth as much as a child's sincere hug or a kiss from a loved one. In the end, it is about accepting life without judgment, knowing each of us is human and that we are all working to face our pain and shadows.

What courage it takes to live this life!

It is a Task I Both Dread and am Grateful For

When I was a young girl, my mother took me to the cemetery on Memorial Day to say prayers for her parents. As I look back, I believe I was in training.

While we were there among the stones, she scolded me if I walked across a grave, a space where a body was buried. I learned respect. She made those spaces seem so real, I must say I also experienced fear that those bodies might rise up and haunt me.

We had so few graves to attend to then, her parents, my grandfather Bruno and the Baby. My Bruno grandparents lost a two-year-old daughter, an aunt to me, that we have forever called The Baby.

Over the years, the number of graves to be honored grew. Joel helps me. It's daunting emotionally, and physically these days, but this is where gratitude comes in. I get to visit with those loved ones. I know they are not there. My task reminds me to talk to them in my head, I remember the gift of love each of them gave me. I leave them a prayer and I use my hands to show my love.

Thich Naht Hanh said: "If you look deeply into the palm of your hand, you will see your parents and all the generations of your ancestors. All of them alive in this moment. Each is present in your body. You are the continuation of each of these people."

Following this ancient custom of honoring ancestors, I live knowing I am well rooted in the cycle of life. Sometimes, it's easy to trip over memories walking the rows. I see the families of friends there, too and remember all we've shared. I rejoice in a time when our family was whole and crowding around the dining room table. I miss them all.

I take comfort in knowing I have no missing parts to my life. I know where I was born, I know who brought me to this place and I know where I will reside in the future. For this I am grateful.

It is a Privilege to Rear a Child.

Your thoughts when that baby is delivered to your arms the moment after taking her first breath turn to wonder for what you and her father have created. It's unbelievable the ecstasy. You think you will be her teacher. You love her beyond anything you know. You keep her safe, guide her, but in the end, **she is your teacher**.

When she goes off to school at five, you ask her how she chooses her friends. She says, "the ones who do good work." She teaches you **children are smarter than you** think.

At a recital alone on stage dancing her version of Bette Midler's *The Rose,* she teaches you about the young **woman emerging from girl with grace**.

When she enters high school and develops new relationships, begins to show independence in her decision-making, she teaches you that **she is her own person on her own journey.**

The day she goes off to college and you drive away sharing your mother's words, "take good care of you for us," you watch the figure of her getting smaller in the distance and your heart pounds in a quandary of joy for opportunity and aching for being separated. She teaches you about **wings.**

Graduation arrives. She's president of her class standing tall before a crowd of peers, professors and parents to deliver her speech. You are bursting your buttons proud. She shares her grandfather's wisdom, "whether life wears a man down or polishes him up depends on the stuff he's made of." She teaches you **about the stuff she's made of.**

In the next moment, before you can catch your breath, she moves to New York City **with no job**. You clench your teeth and have little choice than to go along with it. She teaches you **about determination.**

When your own mother is struggling with terminal illness, your daughter comes home every weekend to help you and her sister care for the grandmother who cared so deeply for them. Her sister and she teach you what **gratitude** really means.

The Stories Wanting to be Told to You

I was sitting in the dealership lounge area one morning waiting for a recall fix on my vehicle. I had my laptop open and was typing when the short wiry man sitting across from me became bored with reading magazines and came to sit by me.

My first thought was "Oh boy, I'm done for now. What's this about? I'm not going to get any work done."

It turned out the surprise was on me.

He had a 1990 vehicle which was in for a sixty thousand miles service. I already had almost fifteen thousand on my vehicle which was only just a year old.

He was ninety years old, spoke with a Scottish brogue. When the service agent came to tell him how much his service would cost, he was very gentle with the agent even though he wasn't going to approve all the repairs because of the cost. I've seen others wanting to shoot the messenger.

We talked about car races. He was quite knowledgeable. I found his stories both engaging and interesting. The one story that stayed with me is about sharing a meal.

He told me that that morning, he gave his wife one hundred dollars so she could take their daughter-in-law and their second son's girlfriend to a sit-down dinner. He was very disturbed that his daughter-in-law never goes out to a nice dinner; she always chooses fast food. He went with her and his granddaughters one day to a fast food chicken place. "Never again!" he exclaimed. "I didn't like it there. I had very nice salmon at a seafood restaurant. I hope they go there. They need to sit down and enjoy a meal."

We talked about war. He was sad when he told me Korea and Viet Nam were worthless wars and the boys paid too high a price.

We talked about alcohol abuse.

We talked about how many friends he's lost.

He neither appeared or acted like ninety years old.

We talked about so many things, always with a

caring, positive perspective.

We actually ended up having quite a nice conversation. I think back of how I could have shut him out, but I'm glad I didn't. Because it would have been my loss. In fact, I wish I could have more conversations with him. He gave me a gift. He made me think about what's meaningful in this life.

You never know the stories that want to be told to you unless you're open to receiving them.

The Hero Within Us

The following quote came from a newsletter from Spring Farm Cares, an animal sanctuary in Clinton, NY.

We keep hearing people say "we need a hero." The animals have been telling us that the hero we are waiting for is within each of us. We are the ones to make a difference. Each one of us carries the answer. Each of us holds a piece of the magic.

The other evening while I was at my yoga studio, Joel and Luc, our Labrador Retriever/German Shepherd mix got into a little spat.

Luc has a girlfriend next door, a brunette Golden Doodle. He visits her without permission and without being invited. That evening, he wouldn't come home when called.

Joel not only had to go to the neighbor's yard, but when Luc saw Joel, he ran home, yet still wouldn't come into the house. He hid in the bushes. He had an awareness of his misdeeds.

Eventually, he allowed Joel to leash him and lead him in.

When I arrived home, I found an unhappy Joel, and Luc sequestered in the lavatory--the penalty box.

Luc when released wouldn't go near Joel all evening and Joel wouldn't even glance Luc's way.

The next morning it was a totally different story. Luc was delighted to greet Joel and more than ready to play.

Luc is a happy dog all the time (aside from time-outs). We could be gone for two minutes or four days and Luc greets us as if we're the best thing that ever happened to him. He has the magic of happiness in him. As we teach him boundaries and behavior, he teaches us forgiveness and how to connect to our hearts. He teaches us to find the hero within ourselves.

What Brings Us to the Place Where We Are?

We gathered at Battery Park Gardens at the very tip of Manhattan in an elegant airy room with a magnificent view of New York Harbor. Springtime sun danced off the water's surface sending polka dots of light on to the room's walls. It was 2006, five years after 9/11 and not far from where the twin towers had risen skyward.

We were there to celebrate our daughter's birthday, a surprise party her sister spent weeks secretly planning. As I looked around and greeted guests, I stood in admiration of the finesse with which our youngest pulled off every detail from two hundred miles away melding friends and family from her sister's experiences— college, living in the City, work and home. It was more than a birthday party, it was testimony to the bond between sisters. It was also an affirmation of life. Had the maitre d' not greeted us with "are you here for the birthday party," it would have been a total surprise.

I often think I learn more from our children than they learn from me. Together, we have endured profound grief. We have lost loved ones regrettably suddenly and in a course of time, but in the face of such sorrow, these young women continue to teach me to enjoy the moments we share together. They remind me that we're capable of experiencing joy, too. They have taught me to take more opportunities to make the most of our lives.

Looking back at the setting sun that balmy April evening, the sky and sea awash in hues of red and orange, I remember seeing Lady Liberty in the distance, "her lamp lifted beside the golden door." I thought of my grandparents who entered America through this harbor almost a hundred years before. They were "poor...yearning to breathe free... homeless" as the poem goes. Before they left their native country, they had never been on a ship before. They left behind sun, warmth and Fascism for a climate of long, harsh winters and democracy. They sailed stormy seas in terribly uncomfortable quarters with hundreds of other poor immigrants. They did not speak

English and when they arrived on American shores, they had no home to go to. They carried with them a "joie de vivre," youth and strong backs. Those were their assets.

In time, they made their way from Ellis Island and New York City north to the rich farmland of central New York State. They took jobs in factories to earn money to buy their own land. Eventually, they purchased farmland, and houses in the village. Their children worked on their farms after school, spring and fall and all summer long. It was grueling work alongside their parents, much of it spent on their knees planting and harvesting. When those children grew up, they learned to be entrepreneurs, businessmen and landowners. They worked hard. They had children. I am one of those children.

My brothers and I have had the benefit of a comfortable home, good nutrition, fine health care and quality education. We travel at ease within and outside of the United States in cars, in planes, on ships and trains

What gifts we received from our grandparents! The gifts they gave us they bought with their lives, their hope and their labor so that we in turn could share this moment with friends and family marking life in the very place they arrived to America, happy and secure in the place where we find ourselves.

The Place We Come Back To

As I looked up from where I was sitting, I noticed how the sun moved through the windows, how it slid along a table, slipped onto the floor, shimmered against a wall. I realized as I and my family maneuvered through our busy years, this house was the place we always returned to, the place that sheltered us for almost half a century, the place that offered us order in a disorderly world.

I thought about the December night I went for a walk after dinner. It snowed just enough to wrap the house and yard in a soft blanket of white. The sky was a deep cobalt blue behind the peaked roofs. Candles in the windows radiated a warm welcoming glow. I ran back to the house and grabbed my camera, walked again to the street and snapped a picture of our home. How different this house was from the one my husband and I built so many years ago.

We designed and constructed our house on an open plot of farmland. We subcontracted out work we couldn't do and labored through work we could do. We moved in on a hot July day thirteen months after we broke ground. For many months after, we had no curtains or shades, little furniture and cupboards that were more empty than full. A child's wooden slide stood in the family room where a sofa would eventually fill the space. I often sat on the floor leaning up against the slide to watch television.

It took years to grow a lawn and trees. The saplings we planted on our patchwork acre were so skinny they were barely visible. They struggled to stretch their roots through earth that was mostly clay. There was no shade other than when the sun moved to the opposite side of the house. Our yard and the plot adjacent to us had been excavated to subsoil so that the vacant land was rock-hard and void of vegetation. Our children referred to this as "the desert." They played there thinking themselves explorers. Some earth was left bulldozed into mounds. Field grass grew from the piles like sea grass from sand dunes. When I looked out from the living room window, I imagined I lived near the sea. Our driveway was a long stretch of stony gravel where roadrunners liked to lay their speckled eggs. We had few things that mature householders owned. What we did have was space and time to grow.

Eventually, the lawn filled in. Each time we mowed it, cut grass was left to decompose. In time, it enriched the earth making our lawn thick and lush. The trees grew lofty into long arms of shade and strong limbs for climbing. Where we planted flowers for sunny locations, we now looked for plants that would grow in shady areas. We blacktopped the driveway, added a brick walkway and patio. Little by little, furniture came into the house covering empty walls and floor space, furniture that made our lives more comfortable, furniture that harbored the souvenirs of our lives.

As time passed, the house filled with more stuff. Each year a child moved into and out of a dorm or an apartment, the leftovers stayed with us. There were gifts of antiques—rockers, a steamer trunk, wicker chairs—from Mom Arsenault. And then there were the "passings" with favorite things passed down to us—an uncle's fishing basket that held our incoming mail, my brother's dinnerware with enough pieces to host our Christmas Eve crowd, my mother's cherry bench where she and a grandchild sat for Thanksgiving dinners, my aunt's tea set that my parents bought for her on their honeymoon.

I thought, "Long after we leave, these walls will still stand. They will hold our memories. These walls will remember little girls' birthday parties, and dinners for parents, a baptism for a godchild, birthday celebrations for a brother and his young son, a post-wedding breakfast for a niece. This house will remember holiday celebrations—stockings hung by the fireplace; Easter egg hunts; Christmas Eves of rolling up the rug to swing dance; Thanksgivings with Papa's special stuffing; New Year's Eve parties with children enjoying special snacks and ginger ale toasts; countless cozy nights under a quilt watching movies on television; soft summer days collecting berries, riding bicycles, reading library books; autumn afternoons collecting fallen leaves; This house will remember children running off the school bus, dogs running *after* the school bus. It will remember our coming home after being away, our rejoicing over a new baby, our healing when we were ill and our grieving after losing loved ones."

I looked around. In my mind's eye, I saw some of those memories—our preschooler in the kitchen cranking the food mill helping me to preserve tomatoes, my husband carrying our teenager upstairs to her room after knee surgery. I heard the squeals of young girls roller-skating in the basement when there was only bare concrete walls and floor. I saw my mother at the nook table rolling out homemade gnocchi, my father in the family room settling into an easy chair reading the newspaper. In the bedrooms, I saw our children sleeping and growing taller. As I approached the hallway, I noticed my husband, briefcase in hand, coming home for dinner. On the lawn, I saw our nephew creating snow sculptures. I heard Mac first, then Zoe, Rocky, Beans, Cashy and now Luc and Max in turn barking to alert me that someone has approached the yard. At the door, I saw them all—aunts, uncles, brothers, cousins, nieces and nephews arriving to party. In the dining room, I saw all the chairs filled.

I thought, "As we grew through these many years, this house evolved, too—a new roof, carpet removed, hardwood floors installed, bookshelves built in, drapes hung, landscaping planted. Yet, the bones of the house stayed the same, stayed strong and steadfast through wind, rainstorms, blizzards and blistering sun. It stood unwavering, waiting—waiting always to welcome us back each time we left."

What I Have Learned From Birthdays

As a youth, it seemed I couldn't get to one place or another fast enough—on foot, on my bike, in a car, a train or a jet plane.

I wanted to change the world or in the very least correct some major flaws within it. I thought I could fix anything. Make everything better. I was going to make an impact.

It's not that way now.

Wisdom seeps in slowly. After all these decades, I savor the moment at hand, I am grateful to have each one, content to be where I am.

I am learning to live without expectation. Expectation leads to disappointment.

I am learning to accept that which I cannot fix or change.

I acknowledge the joints who shout at me at times and offer this advice to youth—enjoy your knees and shoulders, ankles, toes, wrists and fingers. Yes, test your strength and flexibility, your muscles and energy, but be mindful to care for those movable, parts too.

I am learning to honor each day, to be grateful for my breath which so often I take for granted. It is my life force.

I rejoice in each sunrise, the light that dispels darkness. When darkness comes, I revel in the quiet, believing that the sun will rise yet again.

When I move up a digit, I mark it with gratitude and celebration for living this life.

Rumi wrote "The breeze at dawn has secrets to tell you. Don't go back to sleep."

I'm awake. I am listening.

A note of gratitude to you, the reader.
Thank you for sharing this time and space with me.

Lorraine Bruno Arsenault's sense of poetry grew from her love of music. Her first job as a youngster was creating a library of vinyl records used in her family's jukebox business. As an undergrad, she traveled on a ship around the world where she became fascinated with Japanese meditation gardens. Today, she's a mom, businesswoman, yoga teacher, poet, author and energy healer. Her writings often reflect her belief that there is more to life than what's before our eyes. Her work has appeared in *Chicken Soup for the Soul*, *Comstock Review* and *Healing Muse*. She co-edited *In the Company of Women* an Anthology Commemorating the 90th Anniversary of the CNY Branch of the NLAPW and is the author of *The Long Run Home* (Foothills Publishing.) She lives in New York State with her husband and a happy, big black dog.

www.ingramcontent.com/pod-product-compliance
Lightning Source LLC
Chambersburg PA
CBHW031217120626
46545CB00003B/884

* 9 7 8 1 9 5 7 2 2 1 0 6 9 *